*Greater Than a Tourist
Ebook and Audiobook fc

Greater Than a Tourist Book Series Reviews from Readers

I think the series is wonderful and beneficial for tourists to get information before visiting the city.

-Seckin Zumbul, Izmir Turkey

I am a world traveler who has read many trip guides but this one really made a difference for me. I would call it a heartfelt creation of a local guide expert instead of just a guide.

-Susy, Isla Holbox, Mexico

New to the area like me, this is a must have!

-Joe, Bloomington, USA

This is a good series that gets down to it when looking for things to do at your destination without having to read a novel for just a few ideas.

-Rachel, Monterey, USA

Good information to have to plan my trip to this destination.

-Pennie Farrell, Mexico

Great ideas for a port day.

-Mary Martin USA

Aptly titled, you won't just be a tourist after reading this book. You'll be greater than a tourist!

-Alan Warner, Grand Rapids, USA

Even though I only have three days to spend in San Miguel in an upcoming visit, I will use the author's suggestions to guide some of my time there. An easy read - with chapters named to guide me in directions I want to go.

-Robert Catapano, USA

Great insights from a local perspective! Useful information and a very good value!

-Sarah, USA

This series provides an in-depth experience through the eyes of a local. Reading these series will help you to travel the city in with confidence and it'll make your journey a unique one.

-Andrew Teoh, Ipoh, Malaysia

>TOURIST

GREATER THAN A TOURIST- LOUISVILLE KENTUCKY USA

E. Murphy

Greater Than a Tourist- Louisville Kentucky USA Copyright © 2023 by CZYK Publishing LLC. All Rights Reserved.

All rights reserved. No part of this book may be reproduced in any form or by any electronic or mechanical means including information storage and retrieval systems, without permission in writing from the author. The only exception is by a reviewer, who may quote short excerpts in a review.

The statements in this book are of the authors and may not be the views of CZYK Publishing or Greater Than a Tourist.

First Edition

Cover designed by: Ivana Stamenkovic

Cover Image: https://pixabay.com/photos/usa-america-kentucky-statue-1641360/

Image 1: By Don Sniegowski - Imported from 500px (archived version) by the Archive Team. (detail page), CC BY 3.0, https://commons.wikimedia.org/w/index.php?curid=74048552

Image 2: By Censusdata - http://en.wikipedia.org/wiki/Image:Fourthstreetlive-ad.jpg, Public Domain, https://commons.wikimedia.org/w/index.php?curid=3706286

Image 3: By Censusdata at en.wikipedia, CC BY-SA 3.0, https://commons.wikimedia.org/w/index.php?curid=18214144

Image 4: CC BY 2.0, https://commons.wikimedia.org/w/index.php?curid=917301

CZYK Publishing Since 2011.
CZYKPublishing.com
Greater Than a Tourist
Mill Hall, PA
All rights reserved.
ISBN: 9798387783067

>TOURIST

50 TRAVEL TIPS FROM A LOCAL

>TOURIST

BOOK DESCRIPTION

With travel tips and culture in our guidebooks written by a local, it is never too late to visit Kentucky . Greater Than a Tourist-Louisville Kentucky USA by author E. Murphy offers first-hand and personal insight into the best ways to visit the Derby City. Most travel books tell you how to travel like a tourist. Although there is nothing wrong with that, as part of the 'Greater Than a Tourist' series, this book will give you candid travel tips from someone who has lived at your next travel destination. This guide book will not tell you exact addresses or store hours but instead gives you knowledge that you may not find in other smaller print travel books. Experience cultural, culinary delights, and attractions with the guidance of a Local. Slow down and get to know the people with this invaluable guide. By the time you finish this book, you will be eager and prepared to discover new activities at your next travel destination.

Inside this travel guide book you will find:
  Visitor information from a Local
  Tour ideas and inspiration
  Valuable guidebook information

Greater Than a Tourist- A Travel Guidebook with 50 Travel Tips from a Local. Slow down, stay in one place, and get to know the people and culture. By the time you finish this book, you will be eager and prepared to travel to your next destination.

>TOURIST

OUR STORY

Traveling is a passion of the Greater than a Tourist book series creator. Lisa studied abroad in college, and for their honeymoon Lisa and her husband toured Europe. During her travels to Malta, an older man tried to give her some advice based on his own experience living on the island since he was a young boy. She was not sure if she should talk to the stranger but was interested in his advice. When traveling to some places she was wary to talk to locals because she was afraid that they weren't being genuine. Through her travels, Lisa learned how much locals had to share with tourists. Lisa created the Greater Than a Tourist book series to help connect people with locals. A topic that locals are very passionate about sharing.

>TOURIST

TABLE OF CONTENTS

Book Description
Our Story
Table of Contents
Dedication
About the Author
How to Use This Book
From the Publisher
WELCOME TO > TOURIST

WHAT TO EXPECT
LOUISVILLE

---

1. LOO-uh-vull
2. Bourbon, Bourbon, Bourbon
3. Off to the Races
4. Hey, Batter Batter
5. Go Cards
6. The River Delivers
7. Won't You Be My Neighbor

NEIGHBORHOODS

8. Old Louisville
9. NuLu
10. Butchertown
11. Highlands
12. Germantown
13. St. Matthews
14. Downtown

RESTAURANTS

15. Jack Fry's
16. The Mayan Cafe
17. Proof on Main
18. Decca
19. Milkwood
20. Butchertown Grocery
21. Hammerheads
22. Holy Grale
23. Harvest
24. The Fat Lamb
25. Feast BBQ

\>TOURIST

DISTILLERIES

26. Bulleit Frontier Whiskey Experience
27. Evan Williams Bourbon Experience
28. Kentucky Peerless Distilling Co.
29. Old Forester Distillery
30. Angel's Envy Distillery
31. Michter's Distillery

THINGS TO DO

32. Go to the Kentucky Derby
33. Explore the Bourbon Trail
34. Visit the Louisville Slugger Museum and Factory
35. Visit the Big Four Bridge
36. Visit the Muhammad Ali Center:
37. Take a tour of the Kentucky Derby Museum
38. Attend the Kentucky State Fair
39. Visit the Louisville Zoo
40. Take a tour of Churchill Downs
41. Explore the Louisville Mega Cavern
42. Go to a concert at the KFC Yum! Center
43. Attend a Louisville City FC soccer game
44. Visit the Thomas Edison House
45. Check out the Speed Art Museum
46. Explore the Belle of Louisville riverboat

PLACES TO STAY

47. The Brown Hotel
48. Omni Louisville Hotel
49. 21c Museum Hotel
50. The Seelbach Hilton Louisville

TOP REASONS TO BOOK THIS TRIP
Packing and Planning Tips
Travel Questions
Travel Bucket List
NOTES

>TOURIST

DEDICATION

This book is dedicated to my fiancé. Thank you for always supporting my wildest dreams!

>TOURIST

ABOUT THE AUTHOR

E is a fiancé, daughter, and dog mom who has spent 7 years in the Derby City, exploring the restaurants, parks, and cultural landmarks of Louisville. When she's not writing, E enjoys spending time with her family and dog.

\>TOURIST

HOW TO USE THIS BOOK

The *Greater Than a Tourist* book series was written by someone who has lived in an area for over three months. The goal of this book is to help travelers either dream or experience different locations by providing opinions from a local. The author has made suggestions based on their own experiences. Please check before traveling to the area in case the suggested places are unavailable.

Travel Advisories: As a first step in planning any trip abroad, check the Travel Advisories for your intended destination.
https://travel.state.gov/content/travel/en/
traveladvisories/traveladvisories.html

>TOURIST

FROM THE PUBLISHER

Traveling can be one of the most important parts of a person's life. The anticipation and memories that you have are some of the best. As a publisher of the Greater Than a Tourist, as well as the popular *50 Things to Know* book series, we strive to help you learn about new places, spark your imagination, and inspire you. Wherever you are and whatever you do I wish you safe, fun, and inspiring travel.

Lisa Rusczyk Ed. D.
CZYK Publishing

>TOURIST

WELCOME TO
> TOURIST

>TOURIST

Louisville Lights

Fourth Street Live! - Louisville

Hills south of Iroquois Park #2

Highlands district, specifically the Bonnycastle neighborhood

>TOURIST

"The world is a book and those who do not travel read only one page."

- St. Augustine

Louisville, Kentucky - a vibrant city located in the heart of the Bluegrass State. Known for its rich history, world-famous bourbon, and iconic horse races, Louisville offers visitors a unique blend of southern hospitality and urban charm. Whether you're here to explore the city's many museums and cultural attractions, sample the local cuisine, or simply soak up the lively atmosphere, you're sure to find something to love about this dynamic and diverse city. From the historic neighborhoods of Old Louisville and Butchertown to the trendy shops and restaurants of NuLu, Louisville has something for everyone. So pack your bags, grab your camera, and get ready to experience all that this exciting city has to offer.

Louisville
Kentucky, USA

Louisville Kentucky Climate

	High	Low
January	40	25
February	46	28
March	59	39
April	70	47
May	78	56
June	86	66
July	89	70
August	88	68
September	82	62
October	70	49
November	57	40
December	47	32

GreaterThanaTourist.com

Temperatures are in Fahrenheit degrees.
Source: NOAA

>TOURIST

WHAT TO EXPECT

Here are some of the things you can expect when visiting Louisville:

Bourbon - Louisville is located in the heart of bourbon country and is home to some of the best distilleries in the world. You can expect to find numerous bourbon-themed attractions, including the Kentucky Bourbon Trail, where you can tour distilleries and taste different types of bourbon.

Before you visit, be sure to pick up a Bourbon Trail Passport and Field Guide! You can pick one up at participating distilleries. The Bourbon Trail Passport is the ultimate guide to exploring the Kentucky Bourbon Trail, a famous tourist attraction in the state of Kentucky. This passport provides a map of the trail, which includes a variety of bourbon distilleries, each with its unique history and signature drink. The passport also offers exclusive discounts and special offers at participating distilleries. Visitors can collect stamps from each distillery they visit, making it a fun way to track their progress along the trail. The Bourbon Trail Passport is a must-have for anyone visiting Kentucky who wants to experience the best of the state's bourbon culture.

Horse Racing - Louisville is also known for the Kentucky Derby, which is held annually at Churchill Downs. During the racing season, you can expect to find a festive atmosphere and exciting events surrounding the derby.

The Kentucky Derby is often referred to as the "most exciting two minutes in sports." This is because the actual horse race typically lasts only about two minutes! Despite its short duration, the Kentucky Derby is one of the most widely watched and anticipated horse races in the world, with millions of viewers tuning in each year to watch the "Run for the Roses." The tradition of awarding roses to the winner of the Kentucky Derby dates back to the very first running of the race in 1875. According to legend, a fashion-savvy socialite named E. Berry Wall presented a bouquet of roses to the winning jockey at the first Kentucky Derby. The rose quickly became associated with the race, and in 1896, the red rose was officially adopted as the Kentucky Derby's official flower. Today, the winner of the Kentucky Derby is draped in a blanket of over 400 red roses, known as

>TOURIST

the "Garland of Roses. The tradition of awarding roses to the winner of the Kentucky Derby remains one of the most iconic and beloved traditions in horse racing, and it is a true honor for any jockey to be presented with the Garland of Roses on the winner's podium. The Kentucky Derby is steeped in tradition, from the colorful hats worn by spectators to the playing of "My Old Kentucky Home" before the start of the race.

Food Scene - Louisville has a vibrant food scene, with a mix of traditional southern cuisine and modern culinary offerings. You can expect to find a wide range of restaurants, from BBQ joints to fine dining establishments.

The city's cuisine is often described as "Southern with a twist," blending traditional southern dishes with international flavors and modern techniques. Louisville has a long history of farming and agriculture, which has shaped its food scene over the years. In the early 1900s, the city was known for its regional specialties like the "Hot Brown" sandwich, a local favorite that consists of turkey, bacon, and Mornay sauce served over toast.

Over the years, Louisville has continued to evolve its culinary scene, with a focus on farm-to-table dining and locally-sourced ingredients. Today, the city is home to a vibrant food culture that includes everything from traditional southern fare to cutting-edge cuisine. The NuLu district, in particular, has become a popular destination for foodies, with a variety of restaurants, cafes, and bars showcasing the city's culinary talent.

Louisville also hosts several food-focused events throughout the year, including the Louisville Food & Wine Festival, the Kentucky Bourbon Festival, and the Taste of Louisville. These events celebrate the city's rich culinary heritage and showcase the best of the local food scene. Overall, the food scene in Louisville, KY is a reflection of the city's unique history and culture.

Cultural Attractions - Louisville is home to many cultural attractions, including the Muhammad Ali Center, the Louisville Slugger Museum and Factory, and the Kentucky Science Center. You can expect to find a variety of museums, galleries, and theaters to explore.

>TOURIST

Did you know? Muhammad Ali, born Cassius Clay, is one of the most celebrated and beloved athletes in history. While Ali is known around the world for his boxing career and activism, his impact on his hometown of Louisville, Kentucky is immeasurable. Ali grew up in Louisville and trained at the city's Columbia Gym, where he developed his legendary boxing skills.

Despite facing racism and discrimination in his hometown and beyond, Ali always remained connected to Louisville and gave back to the community throughout his life. He supported a variety of local organizations, including the Muhammad Ali Center, which serves as a museum and cultural center dedicated to his life and legacy. The center celebrates Ali's dedication to social justice, his athleticism, and his contributions to Louisville and beyond.

Today, Ali is celebrated as a hero in Louisville, with a variety of tributes throughout the city. The Muhammad Ali International Airport, located in Louisville, bears his name, and a statue of Ali stands outside the Kentucky Center for African American Heritage. The city also hosts an annual Muhammad

Ali Festival, which celebrates his life and legacy with a variety of events and activities.

Overall, Muhammad Ali is an important figure in Louisville's history and culture, serving as a source of pride and inspiration for the city and its residents. His legacy is a reminder of the power of perseverance, courage, and dedication, and his impact will continue to be felt for generations to come.

Outdoor Activities - Louisville has many parks and outdoor spaces to explore, including the Louisville Waterfront Park, Olmsted Parks, and Cherokee Park. You can expect to find plenty of opportunities for hiking, biking, and other outdoor activities.

One of the most popular outdoor destinations in Louisville is Cherokee Park, a scenic urban park designed by renowned landscape architect Frederick Law Olmsted. The park features over 2.4 miles of hiking trails, as well as cycling and horseback riding paths. There are also plenty of opportunities for picnicking, bird-watching, and other outdoor activities in the park.

>TOURIST

Another popular destination for outdoor enthusiasts in Louisville is the Parklands of Floyds Fork, a 4,000-acre park system with over 100 miles of hiking and biking trails. Visitors can explore the park's forests, meadows, and waterways, and enjoy activities like fishing, kayaking, and canoeing.

For those who prefer urban cycling, Louisville has an extensive network of bike lanes and trails that allow cyclists to explore the city's neighborhoods and landmarks. The Louisville Loop is a 100-mile trail that encircles the city, offering a scenic and convenient way to explore Louisville's diverse neighborhoods and attractions.

Overall, Louisville offers a wealth of outdoor activities for visitors and locals alike, with something to suit every interest and skill level. Whether you're looking for a challenging hike, a leisurely bike ride, or a scenic paddle on the water, Louisville has plenty of options to choose from.

>TOURIST

LOUISVILLE

1. LOO-UH-VULL

Louisville is a city with a name that is famously difficult to pronounce. Depending on who you ask, you may hear a variety of different pronunciations. Some locals pronounce it "LOO-uh-vull", while others say "LOO-ee-vill" or "LOO-iss-vill". Visitors may also hear "LOO-uh-vil" or "LOO-vull". Despite the different pronunciations, all variations are generally accepted and recognized as referring to the same city. So whether you're a native or a first-time visitor, don't worry too much about getting the pronunciation exactly right.

2. BOURBON, BOURBON, BOURBON

Bourbon is a big deal in Louisville, Kentucky. Known as the "Bourbon Capital of the World", the city is home to many world-renowned distilleries and bourbon-related attractions. Visitors can take tours of distilleries like the historic Evan Williams Bourbon Experience or the modern Angel's Envy, learn about the history of bourbon at the Frazier History Museum, or sample a variety of bourbons at local bars and restaurants. The city also hosts several bourbon-themed events throughout the year, including the Kentucky Bourbon Festival and the Bourbon & Beyond music festival.

3. OFF TO THE RACES

Horse racing is an integral part of Louisville's culture and history. Home to the world-famous Kentucky Derby, the city has a long and proud tradition of horse racing that dates back to the 1800s. Each year, thousands of visitors flock to Churchill Downs to witness the "most exciting two minutes in sports" and soak up the lively atmosphere of the Derby. In addition to the Kentucky Derby, the city also hosts several other horse racing events throughout the year, including the Kentucky Oaks and the Breeders' Cup. Whether you're a die-hard racing fan or simply interested in experiencing this unique and exciting event, the Kentucky Derby and horse racing in Louisville are not to be missed.

4. HEY, BATTER BATTER

The Louisville Slugger is an iconic baseball bat that has been used by some of the game's greatest players for over a century. Made by the Hillerich & Bradsby Company in Louisville, the Slugger is a symbol of American craftsmanship and ingenuity. Outside the museum, you will find the largest baseball bat in the world. Be sure to grab a photo with it!

5. GO CARDS

The University of Louisville is a renowned research university located in Louisville, Kentucky. With over 22,000 students enrolled in undergraduate and graduate programs, the university is a hub of academic activity and innovation. U of L offers a wide range of majors and degree programs, including engineering, business, education, and the arts. The university is also home to several research centers and institutes that focus on topics like cancer research, renewable energy, and spinal cord injuries. In addition to its academic offerings, the University of Louisville is also known for its vibrant campus life, with over 400 student organizations and a strong athletic program that includes NCAA Division I teams. Whether you're a prospective student or simply interested in learning more about one of Kentucky's top universities, the University of Louisville is definitely worth a closer look.

>TOURIST

6. THE RIVER DELIVERS

Louisville is situated on the banks of the Ohio River, one of the most important waterways in the United States. The river has played a crucial role in the development of the city, serving as a major transportation route for goods and people since the early days of settlement. Today, the Ohio River remains a vital part of Louisville's economy, with barges carrying millions of tons of cargo through the city each year.

7. WON'T YOU BE MY NEIGHBOR

Louisville is broken down into many distinct neighborhoods throughout the city. Each of the neighborhoods offers a unique and distinct experience, and visitors are sure to find something to love in every corner of the city. Be sure to research which neighborhood fits your vibe before you travel to the city!

>TOURIST

NEIGHBORHOODS

8. OLD LOUISVILLE

Old Louisville is a historic neighborhood located just south of downtown and close to U of L's campus. Known for its stunning Victorian architecture, Old Louisville is one of the largest preserved historic districts in the United States. Visitors can take a walking tour of the neighborhood to see its beautiful mansions, tree-lined streets, and charming local shops. With over 48 city blocks of preserved historic homes, Old Louisville is one of the largest preserved historic districts in the United States.

9. NULU

Short for "New Louisville", NuLu is a trendy and eclectic neighborhood known for its art galleries, boutiques, and restaurants. Visitors can explore the area's vibrant street art, sample the local cuisine, and browse unique shops and galleries. NuLu is also a foodie's paradise, with a diverse range of restaurants offering everything from farm-to-table cuisine to international fare.

10. BUTCHERTOWN

Butchertown is a historic neighborhood located just east of downtown Louisville. Once home to the city's slaughterhouses and meatpacking industry, Butchertown is now a vibrant neighborhood known for its nightlife, dining, and shopping. Visitors can check out the area's hip bars and restaurants, or browse the boutiques and art galleries along Main Street. Butchertown is also home to several beautiful parks and green spaces, including the Louisville Waterfront Park, which offers stunning views of the Ohio River. One of the highlights of the neighborhood is the Butchertown Market, which features local vendors selling everything from fresh produce to artisanal crafts.

>TOURIST

11. HIGHLANDS

Located just east of downtown, the Highlands is a lively and diverse neighborhood known for its eclectic mix of shops, restaurants, and nightlife. The neighborhood is also home to several beautiful parks, including Cherokee Park, which offers over 400 acres of hiking trails, playgrounds, and picnic areas. Visitors can explore the area's historic homes or check out the many locally owned businesses that call the Highlands home.

12. GERMANTOWN

Germantown is a historic and charming neighborhood located just east of downtown Louisville. Originally settled by German immigrants in the 1800s, Germantown is now a diverse and thriving neighborhood known for its independent businesses, street festivals, and tight-knit community. Visitors can explore the area's unique architecture, which features charming shotgun houses and colorful murals, or enjoy a meal at one of the many local restaurants, which offer everything from traditional

German cuisine to modern farm-to-table dishes. Visitors can also sample the area's many craft breweries and restaurants, or stroll through the neighborhood's beautiful parks and gardens.

13. ST. MATTHEWS

St. Matthews is a bustling and affluent neighborhood located just east of downtown Louisville. Located just east of the Highlands, St. Matthews is a bustling neighborhood known for its upscale shopping and dining options. The neighborhood is also home to several beautiful parks, including Seneca Park, which features walking trails, tennis courts, and a golf course. Visitors can shop at the area's many high-end boutiques and specialty stores, or dine at one of the many acclaimed restaurants that call St. Matthews home.

>TOURIST

14. DOWNTOWN

Downtown Louisville is the beating heart of the city and a hub of cultural and entertainment activity. Visitors can take a stroll along the famous Fourth Street Live! entertainment district, which is lined with trendy restaurants, bars, and shops. The area is also home to several popular cultural institutions, including the Muhammad Ali Center, the Kentucky Science Center, and the Frazier History Museum. Visitors can also explore the city's historic sites, including the Louisville Slugger Museum and Factory, where they can see the iconic Louisville Slugger baseball bats being made. Downtown Louisville is also known for its stunning architecture, including the historic Brown Hotel and the Louisville Palace Theatre. Visitors can also take a stroll along the Ohio River waterfront, which features beautiful parks, public art, and stunning views of the river. Whether you're interested in culture, entertainment, or simply exploring the heart of the city, Downtown Louisville is definitely worth a visit.

RESTAURANTS

Louisville is a foodie's paradise, offering a wide range of dining options from traditional Southern cuisine to international fare. Here's a guide to some of the best restaurants in the city:

15. JACK FRY'S

Jack Fry's is a legendary restaurant that has been serving up classic Southern cuisine in Louisville since 1933. Located in the historic Highlands neighborhood, this iconic eatery is known for its cozy atmosphere, exceptional service, and delicious food. The menu features a variety of Southern favorites, including fried chicken, shrimp and grits, and bourbon-glazed pork chops, as well as an extensive wine list and classic cocktails. The interior of the restaurant is warm and inviting, with wood-paneled walls, a cozy bar, and vintage photos and memorabilia. Jack Fry's has been a favorite of locals and visitors alike for nearly a century, and continues to be a must-visit destination for anyone looking for a taste of classic Southern hospitality in Louisville.

16. THE MAYAN CAFE

The Mayan Cafe is a top-rated restaurant in Louisville that offers a unique and modern take on Mexican cuisine. The menu is inspired by the culinary traditions of the Yucatan region of Mexico, and features locally sourced ingredients that are prepared using traditional techniques. Diners can enjoy dishes such as cochinita pibil (slow-roasted pork), ceviche, and grilled fish, as well as vegetarian and gluten-free options. The restaurant's interior is warm and inviting, with bright colors, rustic wood accents, and beautiful Mexican artwork adorning the walls. The Mayan Cafe is also known for its excellent cocktails and extensive tequila and mezcal selection. With its creative and delicious cuisine, friendly service, and beautiful atmosphere, The Mayan Cafe is a must-visit destination for anyone looking for a unique and memorable dining experience in Louisville.

17. PROOF ON MAIN

Proof on Main is a renowned restaurant located in the heart of downtown Louisville. Known for its upscale atmosphere, exceptional service, and creative cuisine, Proof on Main has become a popular destination for locals and visitors alike. The restaurant features an innovative menu that showcases the best of Southern cuisine, using locally sourced ingredients whenever possible. Diners can indulge in dishes like Buttermilk Fried Chicken, Grilled Pork Chop, or Shrimp and Grits, while also enjoying an extensive wine and cocktail list. The interior of Proof on Main is just as impressive as the food, with a contemporary design that combines sleek, modern lines with rustic details like exposed brick and wooden beams. Whether you're looking for a romantic night out or a special occasion celebration, Proof on Main is sure to deliver an unforgettable dining experience.

>TOURIST

18. DECCA

Decca is a charming restaurant located in the heart of Louisville's NuLu neighborhood. The restaurant is housed in a historic 1870s building that has been beautifully restored and transformed into a chic dining destination. Decca's menu is a celebration of farm-to-table cuisine, featuring locally sourced ingredients from regional farms and purveyors. The menu changes frequently to reflect the seasons and the availability of fresh ingredients but always features creative dishes that showcase the best of Southern cuisine with global influences. Diners can enjoy dishes like the Crispy Duck Leg Confit, Grilled Beef Short Rib, or the Kentucky Silver Carp Crudo. In addition to the food, Decca is known for its extensive wine list, featuring an impressive selection of organic, biodynamic, and natural wines from around the world. The restaurant's warm and inviting interior features an open kitchen, a cozy bar, and a charming courtyard patio, providing a relaxed and intimate atmosphere for guests to enjoy their meals. Whether you're looking for a romantic dinner for two or a night out with friends, Decca is the perfect destination for a memorable dining experience.

19. MILKWOOD

Milkwood is a modern Asian restaurant located in Louisville, Kentucky's vibrant downtown area. The restaurant is the brainchild of Chef Edward Lee, a James Beard Award nominee and fan favorite on TV's "Top Chef." Milkwood's menu is an eclectic fusion of flavors, blending traditional Asian cuisine with Southern ingredients and techniques. Diners can indulge in dishes like Korean Fried Chicken Wings, Miso Braised Short Ribs, or Coconut Curry Noodles, all of which are made with locally sourced ingredients whenever possible. In addition to the food, Milkwood features an impressive selection of cocktails, beers, and wines from around the world, carefully curated to complement the flavors of the cuisine. The restaurant's interior is sleek and modern, with an open kitchen, a chic bar, and a warm and inviting dining room. Whether you're looking for a quick lunch, a leisurely dinner, or a night out with friends, Milkwood is the perfect destination for an unforgettable dining experience.

>TOURIST

20. BUTCHERTOWN GROCERY

Butchertown Grocery is a sophisticated restaurant located in Louisville, Kentucky's historic Butchertown neighborhood. The restaurant occupies a beautifully restored 19th-century brick building, and its chic interior features a mix of classic and modern design elements. Butchertown Grocery's menu offers a refined take on traditional American cuisine, using locally sourced ingredients and seasonal produce to create dishes that are both innovative and comforting. Diners can enjoy dishes like Seared Scallops, Dry-Aged Ribeye Steak, or Buttermilk Fried Chicken, along with an extensive selection of wines, beers, and cocktails. Butchertown Grocery also features a bakery, serving freshly baked bread, pastries, and desserts made on-site daily. Whether you're looking for a romantic dinner for two or a night out with friends, Butchertown Grocery is the perfect destination for an elegant and memorable dining experience.

21. HAMMERHEADS

Hammerheads is a casual and lively restaurant located in Louisville, Kentucky's Germantown neighborhood. The restaurant is known for its creative take on Southern comfort food, with a focus on smoked meats, burgers, and sandwiches. Diners can indulge in dishes like the Smoked Brisket, Pork Belly Tacos, or the Big A** Burger, all of which are made with high-quality ingredients and house-made sauces. Hammerheads also offers an extensive selection of craft beers and cocktails, making it the perfect spot for a night out with friends. The restaurant's interior is cozy and rustic, with a welcoming vibe that invites guests to relax and enjoy their meal. Hammerheads also features a patio area, perfect for outdoor dining during warmer months. Whether you're in the mood for a hearty meal or a casual night out, Hammerheads is the perfect spot for delicious food and a fun atmosphere.

>TOURIST

22. HOLY GRALE

The Holy Grale is a unique restaurant and beer hall located in the heart of Louisville, Kentucky's Highlands neighborhood. Housed in a former church building, the restaurant features a stunning interior with soaring ceilings, stained glass windows, and intricate woodwork. The Holy Grale's menu offers a wide range of dishes, including hearty pub fare like the Holy Grale Burger, as well as more refined options like the Grilled Octopus. However, the real star of the show is the extensive beer list, which features over 30 rotating craft beers on tap, as well as an impressive selection of bottled beers from around the world. The knowledgeable staff is always happy to make recommendations and help guests find the perfect beer to pair with their meal. Whether you're a beer enthusiast or simply looking for a unique dining experience, the Holy Grale is the perfect spot to enjoy great food and drink in a truly one-of-a-kind setting.

23. HARVEST

Harvest is a farm-to-table restaurant located in the heart of Louisville, Kentucky's NuLu neighborhood. The restaurant is committed to using locally sourced ingredients from regional farms and purveyors, and the menu changes frequently to reflect the seasons and the availability of fresh produce. Diners can enjoy dishes like the Kentucky Bison Burger, the Buttermilk Fried Chicken, or the Rainbow Trout, all of which are made with the freshest ingredients possible. Harvest also offers an impressive selection of wines, beers, and cocktails, carefully chosen to complement the flavors of the cuisine. The restaurant's interior is warm and inviting, with an open kitchen, a cozy bar, and a charming patio area perfect for outdoor dining during warmer months. Whether you're looking for a romantic dinner for two or a night out with friends, Harvest is the perfect destination for a delicious and memorable dining experience that celebrates the best of Kentucky's culinary traditions.

>TOURIST

24. THE FAT LAMB

The Fat Lamb is a contemporary Mediterranean restaurant located in the heart of Louisville, Kentucky's historic Highlands neighborhood. The restaurant is owned and operated by Chef Dallas McGarity, who is known for his inventive and flavorful dishes. The Fat Lamb's menu features a mix of traditional Mediterranean cuisine with a modern twist, using locally sourced ingredients whenever possible. Diners can indulge in dishes like the Grilled Octopus, the Lamb Shank, or the Chicken Schnitzel, all of which are made with the freshest ingredients possible. The restaurant also offers an extensive selection of wines, beers, and cocktails, carefully chosen to complement the flavors of the cuisine. The Fat Lamb's interior is sleek and modern, with a chic bar, an open kitchen, and a warm and inviting dining room. Whether you're looking for a romantic dinner for two or a night out with friends, The Fat Lamb is the perfect destination for a delicious and unforgettable dining experience.

25. FEAST BBQ

Feast BBQ is a beloved barbecue joint located in the heart of Louisville's trendy NuLu neighborhood (and a second location in the Jeffersontown neighborhood). The restaurant serves up traditional Southern-style barbecue with a Kentucky twist, featuring smoked meats, savory sides, and homemade sauces that are sure to satisfy even the most discerning barbecue connoisseur. Diners can enjoy dishes like Brisket, Pulled Pork, or Smoked Chicken, all of which are slow-cooked to perfection and served up hot and fresh. Feast BBQ also offers a selection of craft beers, cocktails, and bourbon, making it the perfect spot to kick back and relax with friends. The restaurant's interior is rustic and inviting, with a laid-back vibe that reflects the spirit of Southern hospitality. Whether you're in the mood for a quick lunch or a leisurely dinner, Feast BBQ is the perfect destination for delicious food, great drinks, and a fun atmosphere.

>TOURIST

DISTILLERIES

Louisville, Kentucky is known as the "Gateway to Bourbon Country," and there are several bourbon distilleries located in and around the city. Here's a guide to some of the top bourbon distilleries to visit in Louisville:

26. BULLEIT FRONTIER WHISKEY EXPERIENCE

The Bulleit Frontier Whiskey Experience is a must-visit attraction for bourbon lovers in Louisville, Kentucky. Located in the historic Stitzel-Weller Distillery, the Bulleit Frontier Whiskey Experience offers visitors an immersive journey into the world of bourbon. Guests can take guided tours of the distillery and learn about the history of Bulleit bourbon, from its founding in the mid-1800s to its resurgence in the modern era. Along the way, visitors will see how the bourbon is made, learn about the aging process, and sample a variety of Bulleit's award-winning whiskeys. The experience also includes interactive exhibits, a gift shop, and a tasting bar, where guests can enjoy a handcrafted cocktail or a flight of bourbons. The Bulleit Frontier Whiskey Experience is a unique and educational destination that celebrates the rich history and tradition of Kentucky bourbon, making it a must-visit for any bourbon enthusiast visiting Louisville.

27. EVAN WILLIAMS BOURBON EXPERIENCE

The Evan Williams Bourbon Experience is a one-of-a-kind attraction located in the heart of downtown Louisville, Kentucky. The experience offers visitors an immersive journey through the history of bourbon, from its origins in Kentucky to its modern-day resurgence. Visitors can take guided tours of the distillery, explore interactive exhibits, and even watch a live cooperage demonstration, where skilled craftsmen create the barrels used to age bourbon. Along the way, visitors will learn about the history and production of Evan Williams bourbon, which has been a staple of Kentucky's bourbon culture since 1783. The experience also includes a tasting room, where visitors can sample a variety of Evan Williams bourbons, including limited-edition releases and small-batch whiskeys. The Evan Williams Bourbon

>TOURIST

Experience is an educational and entertaining destination that celebrates the rich history and tradition of Kentucky bourbon, making it a must-visit for any bourbon lover visiting Louisville.

28. KENTUCKY PEERLESS DISTILLING CO.

The Kentucky Peerless Distilling Company is a family-owned bourbon distillery located in Louisville, Kentucky. With over 100 years of history, the distillery is steeped in the tradition and craftsmanship of Kentucky bourbon. Visitors can take guided tours of the distillery, which include a visit to the production floor to see how bourbon is made, as well as a tasting of Kentucky Peerless's award-winning bourbons. The distillery's signature spirit is a small-batch, single-barrel bourbon that is aged for at least four years and bottled at barrel strength. The distillery also offers a rye whiskey and a wheat whiskey, as well as limited-edition releases that are highly sought after by bourbon enthusiasts. The Kentucky Peerless Distilling Company is dedicated to preserving the legacy of Kentucky bourbon and producing high-quality, handcrafted spirits that are a testament to the art and science of distilling. A visit to the distillery is a unique and unforgettable experience that offers a true taste of Kentucky's bourbon culture.

29. OLD FORESTER DISTILLERY

The Old Forester Distillery is a must-visit destination for bourbon lovers in Louisville, Kentucky. Located in the heart of downtown, the distillery offers visitors an immersive experience that combines history, education, and, of course, great bourbon. Visitors can take guided tours of the distillery, which include a visit to the working production floor, where they can see how Old Forester bourbon is made. Along the way, they'll learn about the rich history of the Old Forester brand, which has been producing bourbon in Kentucky for over 150 years. The experience also includes interactive exhibits, a tasting room, and a gift shop, where visitors can purchase bottles of their favorite Old Forester bourbons. The distillery's signature bourbon is a small-batch, single-barrel spirit that is aged for at least four years and bottled at 100 proof. The Old Forester Distillery is dedicated to producing high-quality, handcrafted bourbon and preserving the

>TOURIST

legacy of Kentucky's bourbon culture. A visit to the distillery is a unique and educational experience that celebrates the art and science of bourbon-making.

30. ANGEL'S ENVY DISTILLERY

The Angel's Envy Distillery is a unique and luxurious destination for bourbon enthusiasts in Louisville, Kentucky. The distillery is housed in a stunningly renovated historic building in downtown Louisville and features a state-of-the-art production facility, tasting room, and gift shop. Visitors can take guided tours of the distillery, which include a visit to the working production floor, where they can see how Angel's Envy bourbon is made. Along the way, they'll learn about the unique finishing process that sets Angel's Envy apart from other bourbons, as each batch is aged in ruby port wine barrels to give it a distinctive flavor profile. The experience also includes a tasting of Angel's Envy's signature bourbons, which include a bourbon finished in port wine barrels, a rye whiskey finished in rum casks, and a limited-edition bourbon finished in Japanese Mizunara oak. The Angel's Envy Distillery is dedicated to producing high-quality, handcrafted bourbon that pushes the boundaries of traditional bourbon-making. A visit to the distillery is a luxurious and educational experience that celebrates the art and science of bourbon-making, making it a must-visit destination for any bourbon enthusiast in Louisville.

31. MICHTER'S DISTILLERY

Michter's Distillery is a renowned bourbon distillery located in the heart of downtown Louisville, Kentucky. With a history dating back to the 18th century, Michter's is dedicated to producing premium, small-batch bourbons that are crafted with the highest level of care and attention to detail. Visitors can take guided tours of the distillery, which include a visit to the working production floor and a tasting of Michter's award-winning bourbons, including its flagship Small Batch Bourbon and Single Barrel Bourbon. Michter's also offers a range of other spirits, including rye whiskey, American whiskey, and limited-edition releases that are highly sought after by bourbon enthusiasts. The distillery's commitment to quality and craftsmanship has earned it numerous accolades and awards, making it a must-visit destination for any bourbon lover in Louisville. A visit to Michter's Distillery offers a unique and educational experience that celebrates the art and science of bourbon-making and showcases the rich history and tradition of Kentucky's bourbon culture.

THINGS TO DO

32. GO TO THE KENTUCKY DERBY

Churchill Downs is an iconic American horse racing venue located in Louisville, Kentucky. The highlight of the racing calendar is the Kentucky Derby, an annual event that draws thousands of visitors from around the world. The atmosphere at Churchill Downs during Derby weekend is electric, with a sea of colorful hats and elegant attire creating a festive and lively ambiance. The race itself is a thrilling experience, with the thundering hooves of the horses and the roar of the crowd creating an unforgettable spectacle. Whether you're a seasoned horse racing fan or just looking for a unique cultural experience, a visit to Churchill Downs for the Kentucky Derby is an experience you won't want to miss. In addition to the excitement of the race, visitors can explore the grounds, take in the beautiful scenery, and enjoy delicious food and drinks. From the excitement of the paddock to the thrill of the finish line, Churchill Downs is a must-see destination for anyone looking for an unforgettable Derby experience.

33. EXPLORE THE BOURBON TRAIL

Louisville is known as the gateway to Kentucky's Bourbon Trail, which features several iconic distilleries that offer tours and tastings. Some of the must-visit distilleries in the area include the Bulleit Frontier Whiskey Experience, the Evan Williams Bourbon Experience, and the Angel's Envy Distillery. Be sure to get your Bourbon Trail passport and collect your stamps along the way.

>TOURIST

34. VISIT THE LOUISVILLE SLUGGER MUSEUM AND FACTORY

Visitors to Louisville can tour the Louisville Slugger Museum & Factory to learn about the history of the bat and see how it's made. The museum also features exhibits on some of the game's most legendary players and offers visitors the chance to hold and swing a real Louisville Slugger. A visit to the Louisville Slugger Museum & Factory is a must for any baseball fan or anyone interested in the history of American sports.

35. VISIT THE BIG FOUR BRIDGE

The Big Four Bridge is one of the most popular attractions in Louisville, Kentucky. The bridge spans the Ohio River and connects Louisville with Jeffersonville, Indiana. It was originally built in 1895 as a railroad bridge and was later converted into a pedestrian and bicycle bridge in 2013.

The Big Four Bridge is a great place to take a leisurely stroll or bike ride. There are several access points to the bridge on both the Kentucky and Indiana sides of the river. On the Kentucky side, visitors can access the bridge from Waterfront Park, which also features playgrounds, fountains, and picnic areas. At night, the bridge is illuminated with colorful LED lights, making it a beautiful sight to see. There are also several events that take place on or near the bridge throughout the year, such as concerts, art installations, and festivals.

36. VISIT THE MUHAMMAD ALI CENTER:

The Muhammad Ali Center is a must-visit destination for anyone interested in learning more about the life and legacy of one of the most iconic athletes and social activists of the 20th century. Located in the heart of downtown Louisville, Kentucky, the center is a museum and cultural center dedicated to the memory of Muhammad Ali. Visitors to the Muhammad Ali Center can explore a wide range of exhibits, interactive displays, and multimedia presentations that tell the story of Ali's life, his impact on society, and his enduring legacy. Highlights of the museum include a collection of Ali's personal memorabilia, including his boxing gloves, robes, and championship belts, as well as interactive exhibits that allow visitors to step into the ring and experience the thrill of a boxing match. In addition to its exhibits, the Muhammad Ali Center also hosts a variety of cultural events, film screenings, and educational programs throughout the year, including talks and panel discussions on issues related to race, religion, and social justice.

37. TAKE A TOUR OF THE KENTUCKY DERBY MUSEUM

The Kentucky Derby Museum is a must-visit destination for horse racing enthusiasts and anyone interested in learning about the history and culture of the Kentucky Derby, one of the most iconic events in American sports. Located at Churchill Downs, the historic racetrack that hosts the Kentucky Derby each year, the museum offers a variety of exhibits and interactive displays that tell the story of the race and its place in American history. Visitors to the Kentucky Derby Museum can explore a wide range of exhibits and displays that showcase the history of the race, including memorabilia from past Derby winners, jockeys, and trainers. The museum also features a 360-degree immersive theater experience that takes visitors on a virtual tour of Churchill Downs, as well as a chance to see real thoroughbreds up close in the museum's stables.

38. ATTEND THE KENTUCKY STATE FAIR

Attending the Kentucky State Fair is a beloved tradition for many Louisvillians and visitors alike. Held annually in late August, the fair is a celebration of all things Kentucky, featuring a wide range of exhibits, livestock shows, food vendors, carnival rides, and live music. Visitors to the Kentucky State Fair can explore a variety of exhibits that showcase the state's rich agricultural heritage, including displays of livestock, crops, and handmade crafts. The fair also features a variety of culinary delights, with vendors serving up classic Kentucky dishes like fried chicken, barbecue, and bourbon balls, as well as more exotic fare like fried Oreos and deep-fried Kool-Aid.

>TOURIST

39. VISIT THE LOUISVILLE ZOO

The Louisville Zoo is a beloved attraction for both locals and visitors, offering a fun and educational experience for visitors of all ages. Located in Louisville's popular Audubon neighborhood, the zoo is home to a wide variety of animals from around the world, as well as a range of exhibits and educational programs. Visitors to the Louisville Zoo can explore a variety of habitats and ecosystems, from the lush rainforests of South America to the arid deserts of Africa. The zoo's collection includes more than 1,500 animals from over 130 species, including gorillas, tigers, elephants, and sea lions.

40. TAKE A TOUR OF CHURCHILL DOWNS

Churchill Downs is a world-famous racetrack located in Louisville and home to the annual Kentucky Derby. A visit to Churchill Downs offers a unique and thrilling experience for horse racing fans and anyone interested in Kentucky's rich racing history. Visitors can take a tour of the historic racetrack, which includes access to the trackside area, the paddock, and the Winner's Circle. The tour also includes a visit to the Kentucky Derby Museum, which features interactive exhibits, artifacts, and memorabilia related to the history of horse racing and the Kentucky Derby.

41. EXPLORE THE LOUISVILLE MEGA CAVERN

Louisville Mega Cavern is a unique and exciting attraction located in the heart of Louisville, Kentucky. This underground adventure park offers a variety of thrilling experiences for visitors of all ages, making it a must-visit destination for anyone looking for a fun and unique adventure. Visitors to Louisville Mega Cavern can take part in a range of activities, including

>TOURIST

underground zip-lining, a ropes course, and a tram tour of the caverns. The caverns themselves are a fascinating sight to behold, with a history dating back to the 1930s when they were used as a storage facility for businesses and the U.S. government.

42. GO TO A CONCERT AT THE KFC YUM! CENTER

The KFC Yum! Center is a state-of-the-art arena located in downtown Louisville, Kentucky, and is one of the premier destinations for live concerts and events in the region. The arena boasts a seating capacity of up to 22,000 people and has hosted some of the biggest names in music, from Taylor Swift and Beyoncé to Metallica and Elton John. Attending a concert at the KFC Yum! Center is an unforgettable experience, thanks to its world-class sound and lighting systems and its spacious, modern facilities. The venue offers a range of seating options, including premium seats and suites, and provides easy access to food and drinks.

43. ATTEND A LOUISVILLE CITY FC SOCCER GAME

Louisville City FC is a professional soccer team that competes in the United Soccer League (USL) and is based in Louisville, Kentucky. Attending a Louisville City FC game is a great way to experience the excitement of live soccer in a lively and passionate atmosphere. Games are typically held at Lynn Family Stadium, a state-of-the-art facility located in the Butchertown neighborhood of Louisville. The stadium has a seating capacity of 15,304, making it one of the largest soccer-specific stadiums in the USL.

44. VISIT THE THOMAS EDISON HOUSE

The Thomas Edison House in Louisville, Kentucky, is a historic museum dedicated to the life and work of the famous inventor, Thomas Edison. The house was built in 1850 and was the residence of the inventor for a brief period in 1866, when he worked as a telegraph operator in Louisville. Today, the Thomas Edison House is open to the public as a museum and offers a unique opportunity to explore the life and work of one of the most important inventors in history. Visitors can take a guided tour of the house and see a collection of original Edison artifacts, including his earliest known light bulb, photographs, and personal letters.

45. CHECK OUT THE SPEED ART MUSEUM

The Speed Art Museum is located on the University of Louisville's campus. The museum features a variety of galleries showcasing everything from ancient Egyptian artifacts to contemporary art. Visitors can explore the museum's collection of paintings, sculptures, decorative arts, and more. Whether you're a seasoned art enthusiast or just looking for a fun and educational day out, the Speed Art Museum is sure to be a highlight of any trip to Louisville.

46. EXPLORE THE BELLE OF LOUISVILLE RIVERBOAT

Exploring the Belle of Louisville riverboat is a unique and exciting experience for visitors to Louisville, Kentucky. The Belle of Louisville is one of the oldest operating steamboats in the country, and has been designated a National Historic Landmark. Visitors can board the Belle of Louisville for a variety of river cruises, including sightseeing tours, dinner cruises, and even live music events. As you cruise along the Ohio River, you'll take in stunning views of the Louisville skyline and surrounding natural beauty. On board the Belle of Louisville, visitors can explore the boat's historic interior, including its grand ballroom, ornate staircases, and vintage steam engines. The boat also features a museum exhibit showcasing the history of steamboats and their role in shaping the nation's economy and culture.

>TOURIST

PLACES TO STAY

Louisville offers a variety of accommodation options to suit any traveler's preferences and budget. Here are some popular places to stay in Louisville:

47. THE BROWN HOTEL

This historic hotel is a Louisville landmark and has been welcoming guests since 1923. It features elegant guest rooms and suites, multiple dining options, and a classic lobby bar. The Brown is located in the heart of downtown Louisville, making it a great option for exploring the city.

48. OMNI LOUISVILLE HOTEL

This modern hotel is located in the heart of downtown Louisville and features luxurious guest rooms and suites, a rooftop pool and bar, a full-service spa, and multiple dining options. The Omni is a great option for travelers who want to be in the center of the action. If you enjoy your stay too much, they offer apartment options!

49. 21C MUSEUM HOTEL

This boutique hotel is known for its contemporary art exhibits, which are displayed throughout the property. The 21c features stylish rooms and suites, a restaurant and bar, and a rooftop terrace. It's located in downtown Louisville and is within walking distance of many popular attractions.

50. THE SEELBACH HILTON LOUISVILLE

This historic hotel features stunning Beaux-Arts architecture and luxurious amenities. It has been welcoming guests since 1905 and has hosted many famous guests over the years. The Seelbach is located in downtown Louisville and is a great option for those who appreciate historic charm and elegance.

>TOURIST

TOP REASONS TO BOOK THIS TRIP

Louisville, Kentucky is a vibrant and dynamic city with a wide range of attractions and activities that make it a popular destination for travelers. Here are some of the top reasons to visit Louisville:

Bourbon: Louisville is known as the "Bourbon Capital of the World" and is home to many of the world's most famous bourbon distilleries and experiences.

Food: Louisville has a thriving food scene with a mix of classic southern comfort food and innovative culinary creations.

History: Louisville has a rich history that includes the Civil War, the Underground Railroad, and the Louisville Slugger baseball bat.

Arts and Culture: The city has a vibrant arts and culture scene, with world-class museums, galleries, and performing arts venues.

Sports: Louisville is home to the Kentucky Derby, the most famous horse race in the world, as well as the Louisville Cardinals college sports teams.

Music: The city has a diverse music scene, with everything from bluegrass and country to jazz and rock.

Outdoor activities: Louisville offers plenty of opportunities for outdoor recreation, including hiking, biking, and boating.

Festivals and Events: The city hosts a number of festivals and events throughout the year, including the Kentucky State Fair, Forecastle Festival, and the Louisville Zombie Walk.

Family-friendly activities: Louisville has a variety of family-friendly attractions, including the Louisville Zoo, Kentucky Science Center, and the Mega Cavern.

Friendly people: Last but not least, Louisville is known for its friendly and welcoming people, making it a great place to visit and explore.

>TOURIST

LOUISVILLE FUN FACTS:

In case you missed them along the way, here are some fun facts to tuck away for the next time you're on Jeopardy.

- Louisville is the birthplace of Muhammad Ali, one of the most famous boxers and activists in history.

- The city is also known as the "Gateway to the South" due to its location on the Ohio River.

- Louisville is home to the Kentucky Derby, one of the most famous horse races in the world, which takes place every year on the first Saturday in May at Churchill Downs.

- The Louisville Slugger baseball bat, which is used by professional baseball players all over the world, is made in Louisville.

- The city is home to the world's largest disco ball, which is 30 feet in diameter and weighs over 2,000 pounds.

- Louisville is the birthplace of the cheeseburger, which was invented by a local restaurant owner named Kaelin's in 1934.

- The city has a unique dialect known as "Louisville Speak," which includes phrases like "y'all" and "gonna" that are commonly used in Southern dialects.

- Louisville is home to the world's only underground zip line, located in the Mega Cavern.

- The Belle of Louisville, a steamboat that has been in operation since 1914, is the oldest operating steamboat in the United States.

>TOURIST

- Louisville is also known for its bourbon distilleries, with over 95% of the world's bourbon produced in the state of Kentucky, and many of the top distilleries located in or near Louisville.

- The Louisville Slugger Museum & Factory produces over 1.8 million wooden baseball bats annually.

- The city was named after King Louis XVI of France, in appreciation of his assistance during the American Revolutionary War.

- The Louisville Zoo is home to the largest indoor rainforest in the world, the Gorilla Forest.

- The city is home to the University of Louisville, which was founded in 1798 and is one of the oldest public universities in the United States.

>TOURIST

PACKING AND PLANNING TIPS

A Week before Leaving

- Arrange for someone to take care of pets and water plants.
- Email and Print important Documents.
- Get Visa and vaccines if needed.
- Check for travel warnings.
- Stop mail and newspaper.
- Notify Credit Card companies where you are going.
- Passports and photo identification is up to date.
- Pay bills.
- Copy important items and download travel Apps.
- Start collecting small bills for tips.
- Have post office hold mail while you are away.
- Check weather for the week.
- Car inspected, oil is changed, and tires have the correct pressure.
- Check airline luggage restrictions.
- Download Apps needed for your trip.

Right Before Leaving

- Contact bank and credit cards to tell them your location.
- Clean out refrigerator.
- Empty garbage cans.
- Lock windows.
- Make sure you have the proper identification with you.
- Bring cash for tips.
- Remember travel documents.
- Lock door behind you.
- Remember wallet.
- Unplug items in house and pack chargers.
- Change your thermostat settings.
- Charge electronics, and prepare camera memory cards.

\>TOURIST

READ OTHER GREATER THAN A TOURIST BOOKS

Greater Than a Tourist- California: 50 Travel Tips from Locals

Greater Than a Tourist- Salem Massachusetts USA 50 Travel Tips from a Local by Danielle Lasher

Greater Than a Tourist United States: 50 Travel Tips from Locals

Greater Than a Tourist- St. Croix US Virgin Islands USA: 50 Travel Tips from a Local by Tracy Birdsall

Greater Than a Tourist- Montana: 50 Travel Tips from a Local by Laurie White

Children's Book: Charlie the Cavalier Travels the World by Lisa Rusczyk Ed. D.

> TOURIST

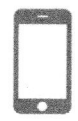

Follow us on Instagram for beautiful travel images:
http://Instagram.com/GreaterThanATourist

Follow *Greater Than a Tourist* on Amazon.

CZYKPublishing.com

> TOURIST

At *Greater Than a Tourist*, we love to share travel tips with you. How did we do? What guidance do you have for how we can give you better advice for your next trip? Please send your feedback to CZYKPublishing@gmail.com as we continue to improve the series. We appreciate your constructive feedback. Thank you.

>TOURIST

METRIC CONVERSIONS

TEMPERATURE

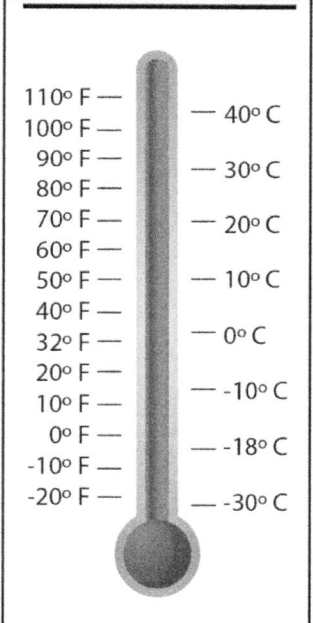

110° F — — 40° C
100° F —
90° F — — 30° C
80° F —
70° F — — 20° C
60° F —
50° F — — 10° C
40° F —
32° F — — 0° C
20° F —
10° F — — -10° C
0° F —
-10° F — — -18° C
-20° F — — -30° C

To convert F to C:
Subtract 32, and then multiply by 5/9 or .5555.

To Convert C to F:
Multiply by 1.8 and then add 32.

32F = 0C

LIQUID VOLUME

To Convert:................Multiply by
U.S. Gallons to Liters............... 3.8
U.S. Liters to Gallons 26
Imperial Gallons to U.S. Gallons 1.2
Imperial Gallons to Liters....... 4.55
Liters to Imperial Gallons 22

1 Liter = .26 U.S. Gallon
1 U.S. Gallon = 3.8 Liters

DISTANCE

To convert ....Multiply by
Inches to Centimeters 2.54
Centimeters to Inches 39
Feet to Meters...................... .3
Meters to Feet 3.28
Yards to Meters 91
Meters to Yards 1.09
Miles to Kilometers 1.61
Kilometers to Miles............ .62

1 Mile = 1.6 km
1 km = .62 Miles

WEIGHT

1 Ounce = .28 Grams
1 Pound = .4555 Kilograms
1 Gram = .04 Ounce
1 Kilogram = 2.2 Pounds

TRAVEL QUESTIONS

- Do you bring presents home to family or friends after a vacation?
- Do you get motion sick?
- Do you have a favorite billboard?
- Do you know what to do if there is a flat tire?
- Do you like a sun roof open?
- Do you like to eat in the car?
- Do you like to wear sun glasses in the car?
- Do you like toppings on your ice cream?
- Do you use public bathrooms?
- Did you bring a cell phone and does it have power?
- Do you have a form of identification with you?
- Have you ever been pulled over by a cop?
- Have you ever given money to a stranger on a road trip?
- Have you ever taken a road trip with animals?
- Have you ever gone on a vacation alone?

>TOURIST

- Have you ever run out of gas?
- If you could move to any place in the world, where would it be?
- If you could travel anywhere in the world, where would you travel?
- If you could travel in any vehicle, which one would it be?
- If you had three things to wish for from a magic genie, what would they be?
- If you have a driver's license, how many times did it take you to pass the test?
- What are you the most afraid of on vacation?
- What do you want to get away from the most when you are on vacation?
- What foods smell bad to you?
- What item do you bring on ever trip with you away from home?
- What makes you sleepy?
- What song would you love to hear on the radio when you're cruising on the highway?
- What travel job would you want the least?
- What will you miss most while you are away from home?
- What is something you always wanted to try?

- What is the best road side attraction that you ever saw?
- What is the farthest distance you ever biked?
- What is the farthest distance you ever walked?
- What is the weirdest thing you needed to buy while on vacation?
- What is your favorite candy?
- What is your favorite color car?
- What is your favorite family vacation?
- What is your favorite food?
- What is your favorite gas station drink or food?
- What is your favorite license plate design?
- What is your favorite restaurant?
- What is your favorite smell?
- What is your favorite song?
- What is your favorite sound that nature makes?
- What is your favorite thing to bring home from a vacation?
- What is your favorite vacation with friends?
- What is your favorite way to relax?
- Where is the farthest place you ever traveled in a car?

>TOURIST

- Where is the farthest place you ever went North, South, East and West?
- Where is your favorite place in the world?
- Who is your favorite singer?
- Who taught you how to drive?
- Who will you miss the most while you are away?
- Who if the first person you will contact when you get to your destination?
- Who brought you on your first vacation?
- Who likes to travel the most in your life?
- Would you rather be hot or cold?
- Would you rather drive above, below, or at the speed limited?
- Would you rather drive on a highway or a back road?
- Would you rather go on a train or a boat?
- Would you rather go to the beach or the woods?

TRAVEL BUCKET LIST

1.

2.

3.

4.

5.

6.

7.

8.

9.

10.

>TOURIST

NOTES

Printed in Great Britain
by Amazon